The Creature Club

The Blue Whale

By Melissa Kim

Illustrated by Shirley Felts

Ideals Children's Books • Nashville, Tennessee

Published by Ideals Publishing Corporation
Nashville, Tennessee 37214

Printed in Hong Kong.

ISBN 0-8249-8614-8 (pap)
ISBN 0-8249-8628-8 (lib)

Conceived, edited, designed, and produced by Signpost Books, Ltd.
Oxford, England OX3 0AB

Editor: Dorothy Wood
Designer: Gillian Riley

Library of Congress Card Catalog # 93-079973
Library of Congress Cataloging-in-Publication Data is available.

The whales need you!

The blue whale—the biggest and most magnificent creature on Earth—has been endangered for many years. Why? Man has hunted the blue whales, and now there are very few left.

By learning about the blue whale and its plight, you can understand more about other whales and perhaps help to preserve the other species of whales that are still in danger—before it's too late and all the great mammals of the sea are only pictures in a book.

If you care about animals in danger, you automatically become a member of The Creature Club—people who share a common concern for animals and want to do something to make the world a better place for the blue whale and for all of us.

3

Are there different types of whales?

The oceans are home to about 80 types of whales. The great whales, as they are commonly called, fall into two groups: baleen whales and toothed whales. The blue whale is one of ten types of baleen whale. Look deep into the mouths of these great creatures and you will see a baleen, or whalebone. Baleens are horny plates, made from the same type of material as your fingernails, and they grow down from the whale's cavernous upper jaw.

Baleen whales move through the oceans, letting gallons of water pass through their mouths. The baleen plates allow the whales to strain food, such as plankton, from the water.

Toothed whales have teeth with which they chew. These whales can eat larger bits of food such as fish and squid.

Here are some of the great whales. Using the descriptions on the facing page, see if you can identify each whale.

Baleen Whales

Right whales have upside-down smiles and grey, white or yellow areas of rough skin on the tops of their heads. These patches are called "callosities" and are usually covered with parasites.

Pygmy right whales are the most streamlined and have no callosities.

Bowhead whales are similar in shape to right whales. They have a very arched upper jaw, but no callosities.

Grey whales are distinctive because of their color.

Humpback whales have many bumps on the tops of their heads and down the lower back. They also have the longest flippers.

Fin whales are sleek and long, with a distinct fin far down their backs and a unique white patch on the right sides of their heads.

Sei whales are long and slim, like fin whales but smaller, and have a single ridge along the tops of their heads.

Minke whales are the smallest of the great whales.

Bryde's whales are similar to Sei whales but have three ridges on the tops of their heads.

Blue whales are the largest of all whales.

Toothed Whales

Sperm whales have teeth and a square head.

How big are blue whales?
They are enormous!

The blue whale is the largest animal that has ever existed on land or sea. Even a baby blue whale is awe-inspiring! At birth it is about 24 ft. (7 m) long. Like humans, blue whales give birth to one baby at a time.

Baby blue whales take about five years to grow into adult whales. By then, a male will be about 72 ft. (22 m) long and a female will be about 79 ft. (24 m) long. Both will grow a a bit more during the course of their adult lives. The average blue whale is between 79 and 92 ft. (24 and 28 m) long. It weighs about 165 tons (about 330,000 lbs. or 150,000 kg). Its tongue alone weighs as much as an elephant!

85 feet

Are whales fish?

No. Whales may be very much bigger than us, but we do have a few things in common with the great creatures of the deep. Like people, whales are mammals. They are warm-blooded, produce milk to feed their young, and have hair on their bodies. Some other sea creatures, like seals and dolphins, are also mammals.

A fish is cold-blooded and lays eggs that hatch instead of giving birth to a baby.

Fish use their gills to breathe under water, but whales breathe air. They come to the surface every now and then to breathe.

The blue whale breathes through a pair of blowholes. Its lungs are specially designed to collapse when it dives deep, so the pressure of the surrounding water is not a problem for the whale as it would be for a human being.

When the whale returns to the surface, its lungs expand again, and the stale air is sprayed out of the blowholes. The blue whale blows out a tall, slender column of spray that is 30 ft. (9 m) high. The spray isn't water; it's vapor, like the spray you breathe out on a cold day.

Whales breathe very efficiently. They empty out and refill almost 90 percent of their lungs. We refill only about 12 percent.

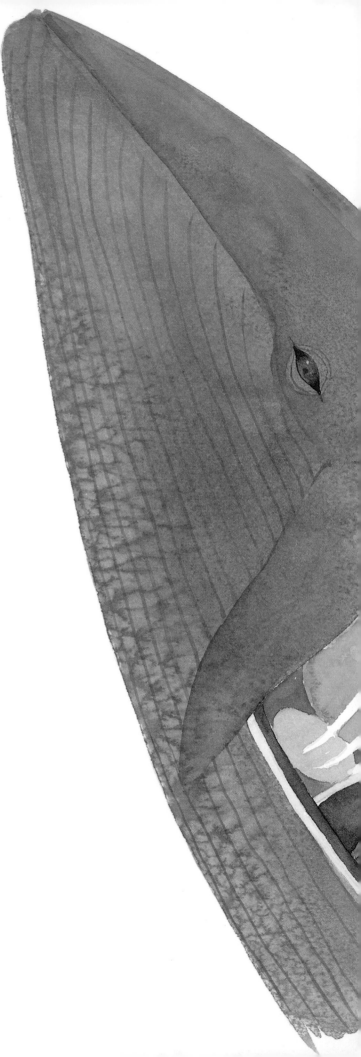

- The bottlenose whale can stay underwater for two hours.

- The sperm whale is the champion deep-diving whale. There are some accounts of dives as deep as 1.8 miles (3 km) underwater!

- The deepest dive by a person holding his breath was achieved by Frenchman Jacques Moyel, who reached a depth of 344 ft. (105 m). It took 194 seconds.

- The deepest dive achieved by a person with scuba equipment was 436 ft. (133 m).

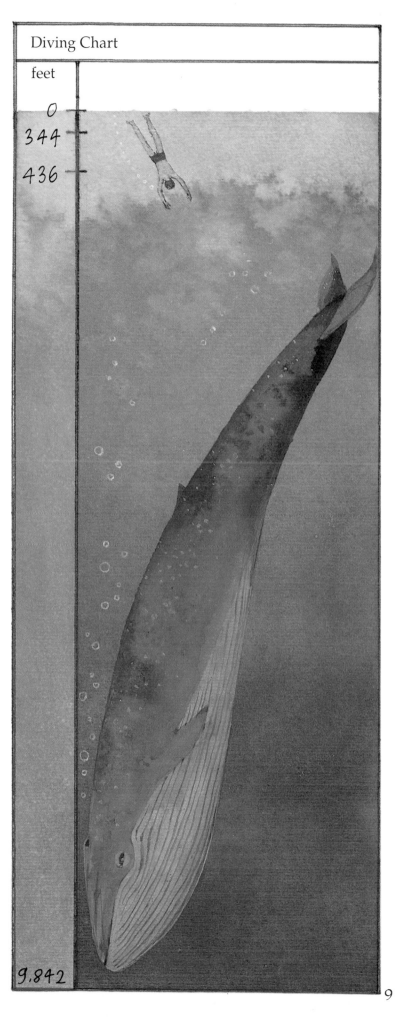

Diving Chart

feet

0

344

436

9,842

9

What do blue whales eat?

Baleen whales feed by licking food off their baleen plates with their tongues. Some trap food on the bristles that line their baleen by swimming along with their mouths open. Others, like the blue whale, take in food with great gulps of water and swish the water out again with their tongues. What's left behind is the blue whale's favorite food—a tiny organism called a **zooplankton**. The blue whale mainly eats a type of plankton called **krill**. Other whales eat a variety of small fish and shellfish as well as plankton.

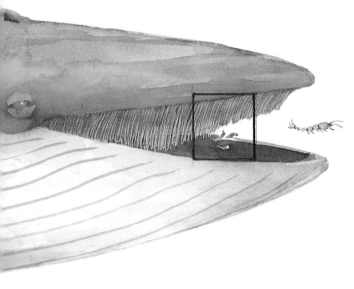

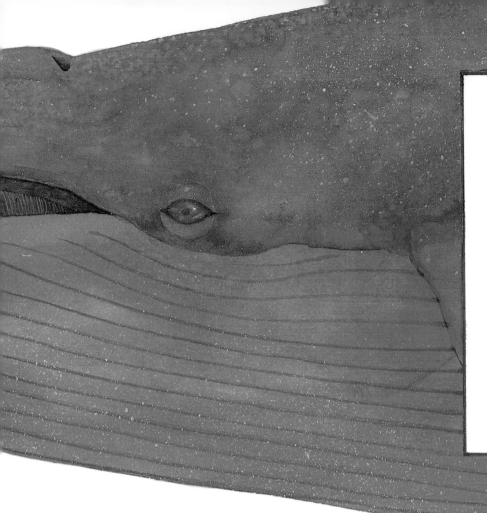

• The blue whale needs to take in about 7,440 pounds—over $3^1/2$ tons—of krill every day!

• The blue whale does most of its feeding in the evening.

• Krill are tiny, weighing only about 1/2 ounce each.

• The blue whale feeds mainly at the surface of the water.

• The blue whale does most of its feeding in the evening.

• The blue whale eats only during the six summer months. In the winter, it migrates to warm places where food is scarce.

CALORIE COUNT

We all eat food to give us energy. The energy value of food is measured in calories. A blue whale needs about 3,000,000 calories a day. If you needed that many calories, how many meals of steak and baked potato, with ice cream as dessert, would you have to eat? Make up some other combinations of food to give you 3,000,000 calories.

Food	Calories per serving
Hamburger	400
Spaghetti	300
Steak	480
Chicken & fries	470
Baked potato	62
Strawberries & cream	180
Ice cream	207

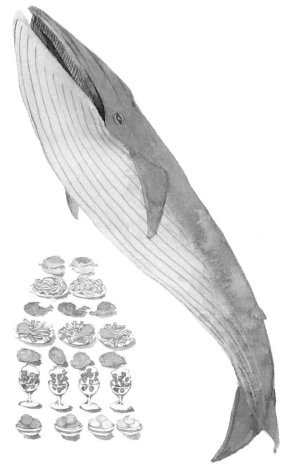

Where do blue whales live?

There are three main groups of blue whales in the world's oceans. One lives in the North Pacific Ocean, one in the North Atlantic Ocean, and one in the southern hemisphere, above Antarctica. It is possible that a fourth group lives in the northern Indian Ocean.

Blue whales don't stay in the same area year round. Where they live at any given time is determined by where they want to have their babies, how cold the water is, and how much food is available.

In the summer months, most blue whales live in the cold northern waters of the Pacific and Atlantic oceans and in the waters off Antarctica. Food is plentiful here, and they eat a lot to store up energy for the long swim they undertake in the winter months. In the winter, most choose to migrate to warmer waters to mate and have babies.

Map of the oceans

Whales must live where they can find food. Many live in the emptier southern seas. This map shows where some groups of whales live. It's very hard to count whale populations, so all numbers are estimates.

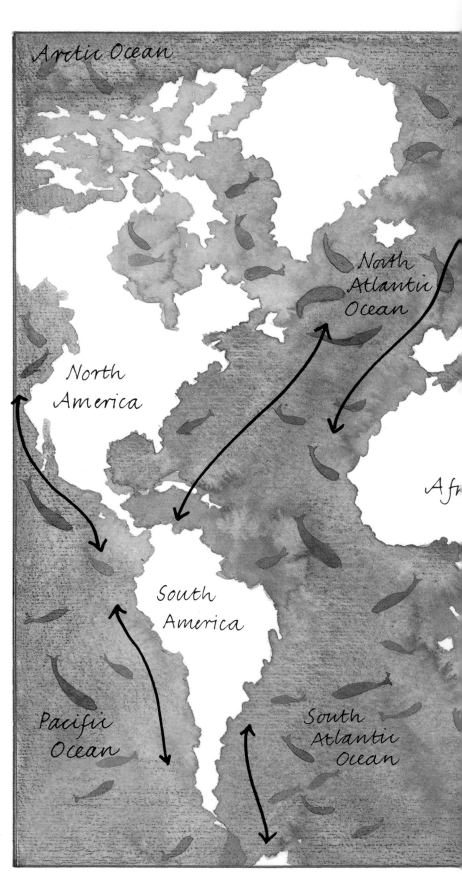

Arctic Ocean

North Atlantic Ocean

North America

Af[r]

South America

Pacific Ocean

South Atlantic Ocean

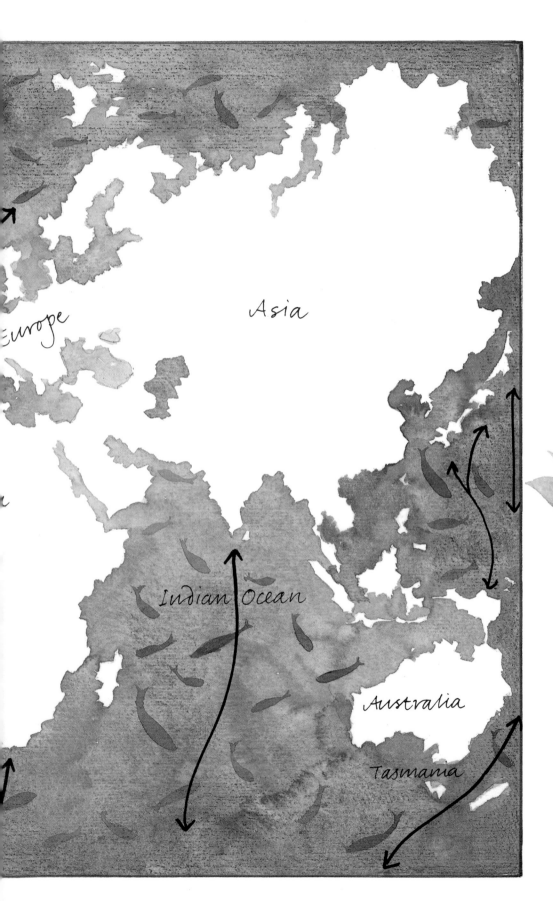

Europe

Asia

Indian Ocean

Australia

Tasmania

KEY

Blue Whale: estimated 11,700; lives in all oceans.

Humpback Whale: 5,500 in N. Atlantic; 1,400 in N. Pacific; 3,000 in southern oceans. An estimated worldwide total of 9,500 to 10,000.

Grey: estimated between 21,500 and 26,500; lives in N. Pacific.

Sei: estimated between 48,000 and 63,000; most live in N. Pacific and southern hemisphere.

Fin Whale: estimated between 105,000 and 121,900; lives in all oceans.

13

What are blue whales like?

Whales are sociable creatures who live in groups that vary in size from two to 100. The blue whale, and most other baleen whales, live in smaller groups. Because they are so big and need so much food, they need to feed on their own, without others competing for the same food. Their size also means they don't have to worry too much about predators.

The sperm whale and other toothed whales live in larger groups. Sperm whales have nursery groups for babies and adult females, bachelor groups for young males, bull groups for adult males, and harems, which have one male and about fourteen females.

Whales have their own special language of chirps, blips, and groans, and they send each other signals through the water. In this way, one whale might tell another about a good place to feed, or even warn off another male who is trying to mate with his female. A sperm whale might use sound to keep his group together.

Whales are very supportive of others in their group. When a group of right whales feels threatened, the members form a tight circle and slap their tails hard against the water. Sperm whales protect an injured whale by forming a circle around it in the shape of a bicycle wheel.

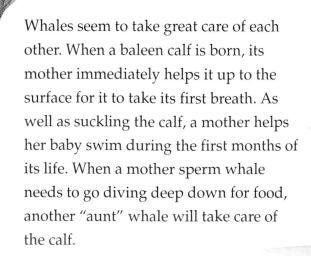

Whales seem to take great care of each other. When a baleen calf is born, its mother immediately helps it up to the surface for it to take its first breath. As well as suckling the calf, a mother helps her baby swim during the first months of its life. When a mother sperm whale needs to go diving deep down for food, another "aunt" whale will take care of the calf.

FACT FILE

How can you tell how old a whale is? If you cut a tree in half, the number of rings inside equals the number of years it has grown. Scientists have found a similar trait in whales.

Baleen whales have ear plugs deep inside their heads, and these plugs have bands of dark and white layers. Each pair of dark and light layers equals one year of growth.

How old is the whale that this ear plug belongs to?

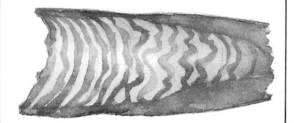

The whale not only has the biggest body and biggest brain of any mammal, it can also make the loudest noise! Every now and again, the blue whale lets out a moan or a groan.

Some whales and dolphins have been known to help man by saving drowning swimmers and leading boats to a safe port.

Whale's milk is very rich. It is 40 to 50 percent fat, while a cow's milk is only five percent fat.

Whales can get sunburned! The skin on the tops of their backs peels off after they've been in the sun too long.

Grey whales are very curious. They don't mind human contact and will let people pet them. They swim up to people in whalewatching boats to investigate the humans.

Toothed whales "see" with their ears, or echolocate (ECK-oh-low-KAT). It's like radar—the whales send out clicks and creaks and listen to the echoes as the sounds bounce off objects in the ocean. They can even tell one kind of fish from another this way.

Humpback whales are the musicians of the ocean. They sing songs that are long, complex, and harmonious.

How can you tell one whale from another?

The grey whale sticks its nose straight out of the water and turns in a slow circle to survey its surroundings. This is called "spy-hopping."

The right whale has lots of callosities or bumps on its head and even has hairs on its chin!

The humpback whale has a very distinctive tail fluke, or tip of the tail. Each has a unique black-and-white pattern.

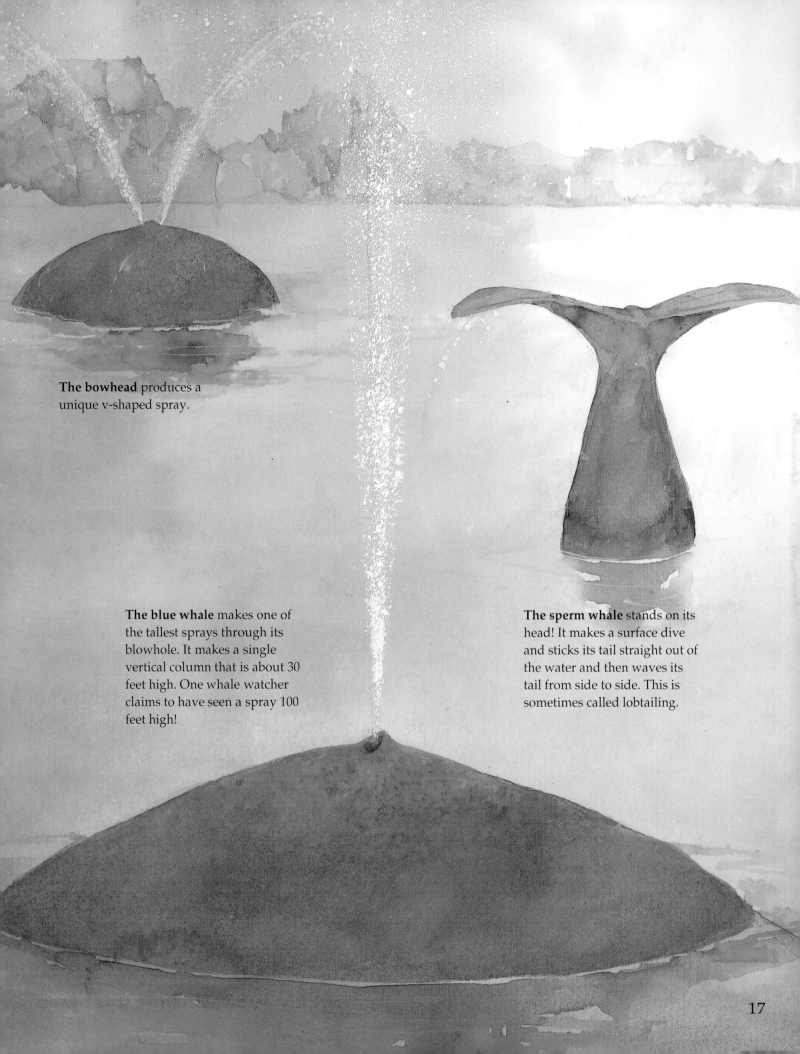

The bowhead produces a
unique v-shaped spray.

The blue whale makes one of
the tallest sprays through its
blowhole. It makes a single
vertical column that is about 30
feet high. One whale watcher
claims to have seen a spray 100
feet high!

The sperm whale stands on its
head! It makes a surface dive
and sticks its tail straight out of
the water and then waves its
tail from side to side. This is
sometimes called lobtailing.

Is the blue whale still endangered?

Yes. Although there has been a worldwide ban on hunting blue whales since 1967, there are so few left that their population may never fully recover. The blue whale's great size, the very thing that enchants us today, also appealed to the greed of hunters.

In the 1900s, whalers started to regulate the number and types of whales they killed. In the 1930s, they came up with the idea of the blue whale unit, based on the amount of oil one blue whale could produce. Whalers were allowed to take 16,000 blue whale units a year. They would hunt the biggest whales first, as they were the most profitable. By the 1960s, the blue whale population had been reduced from about 300,000 to about 14,000.

110 barrels of oil=

1 blue whale =
2 fin whales=
2 $\frac{1}{2}$ humpback whales=
6 sei whales

Grenade harpoon invented in Norway; marks start of modern whaling

First modern factory whaling ship goes into operation; so whales can now be processed on board at sea

Blue whale unit adopted

Ban on commercial whaling of right, bowhead, and grey whales

Formation of IWC

1868

1925

1931

1935

1946

Are all whales protected?

International laws exist protecting almost all the different types of whales. The CITES treaty (the Convention on International Trade in Endangered Species), which came into effect in 1975 to prevent trade in endangered animals and plants, restricts trade in products made from the blue whale, the sei whale, and the minke whale.

The International Whaling Commission, or IWC, specifically regulates the whaling industry. The IWC was formed in 1946 by the whaling nations. Its goals then were to set quotas, or limits, on the number of whales each nation could kill, to set the whaling seasons, and to protect baby whales and nursing mothers. As public pressure to save the whales grew, the IWC was forced to take steps to halt commercial whaling altogether.

In 1985 all commercial whaling was banned for five years. In 1990, 1991, and 1992, the nations met and decided to extend the ban for another year. This doesn't mean that whales are safe from hunters. Countries can still kill whales for scientific research or for local consumption. Whalers from Japan, Iceland, and Norway continue to kill minke, sei, and fin whales. They claim it is to study whales, but often they sell the whale meat.

Iceland has now dropped out of the IWC, and Norway plans to resume commercial whaling in 1993. The IWC has no legal power to enforce its laws, so whales, far from safe, must rely on the good will of nations to abide by the rules.

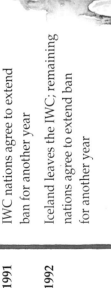

1966	1967	1972	1972	1973	1979	1980	1985	1986	1991	1992
Ban on commercial whaling of humpback whales	Ban on commercial whaling of blue whales	Dropping of the blue whale unit	US passes Marine Mammal Protection Act to help whales and dolphins	Start of the "Save the Whale" campaign which includes boycotts on products from whaling nations and companies using sperm whale oil	Indian Ocean Sanctuary established	European nations adopt ban on sperm whale oil and all whale products	Ban on commercial whaling of sperm whales	Five-year ban on all commercial whaling begins	IWC nations agree to extend ban for another year	Iceland leaves the IWC; remaining nations agree to extend ban for another year

How are whales caught?

A

The first records of whaling date from the 10th century. People in Alaska and Norway went out in open boats with handmade spears to attack the slowest whales—the grey, right, and bowhead.

B

Other early whalers tried to drive whales ashore. Once on land, the whales would die, crushed by the weight of their own bodies. The right whale got its name because it was the "right" whale to hunt—it swam slowly, it floated once it was killed (and therefore was easy to drag ashore), and it produced lots of oil and meat.

C

In 1868 a Norwegian named Svend Foyn invented an explosive grenade harpoon. This harpoon was shot from a cannon mounted onto the whaling boat. Once inside the whale's skin, the harpoon tip would explode like a bomb.

D

Foyn also tackled another problem. Several types of whales, such as the humpback, don't float once they are killed, so they are very hard to recover. Foyn invented the inflation lance, a type of hollow spear. Once the lance had killed the whale, the whaler could blow air through it and inflate the whale to make it float.

E

Also at this time, steamships replaced sailing ships. Whalers could now race after whales, secure the dead whales to the boat, and tow them away. Then, in 1925, factory ships enabled whalers to process dozens of whale carcasses while at sea. Modern whaling had truly begun.

Why are whales hunted?

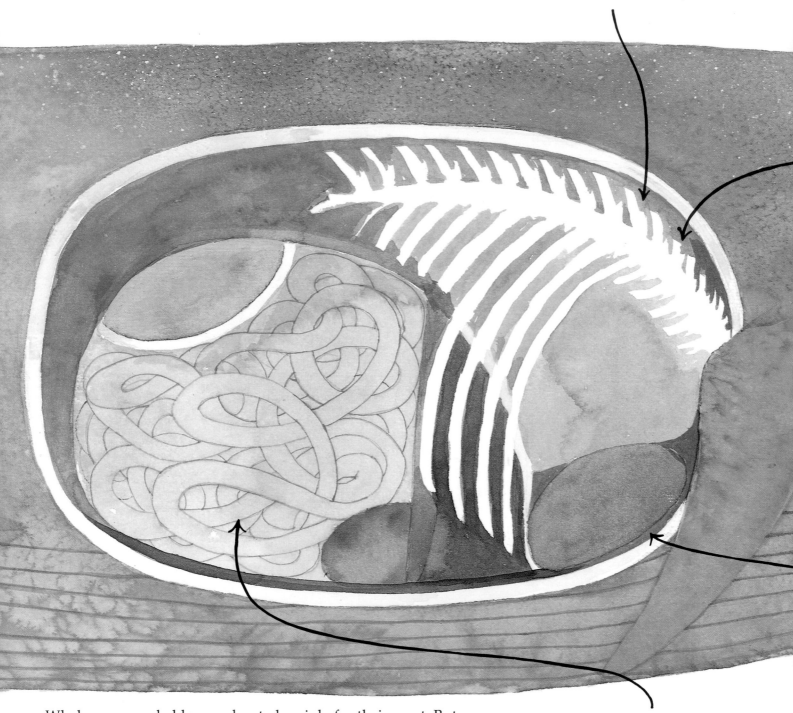

In the 1950s, whale meat—by-products from different parts of the whale—was used to make fodder and fertilizer.

Whales were probably once hunted mainly for their meat. But the most desirable commercial product from whales was, and is, their oil. Whale oil and blubber were boiled to get an extract that could be used as fuel or fat. Ironically, as commercial whaling dies down, whales are once again being killed mainly for their meat.

The intestines of the sperm whale can be used to make ambergris, a fatty substance which gives off a pleasant smell when burned. Ambergris was used in religious ceremonies and was also sold as an expensive perfume.

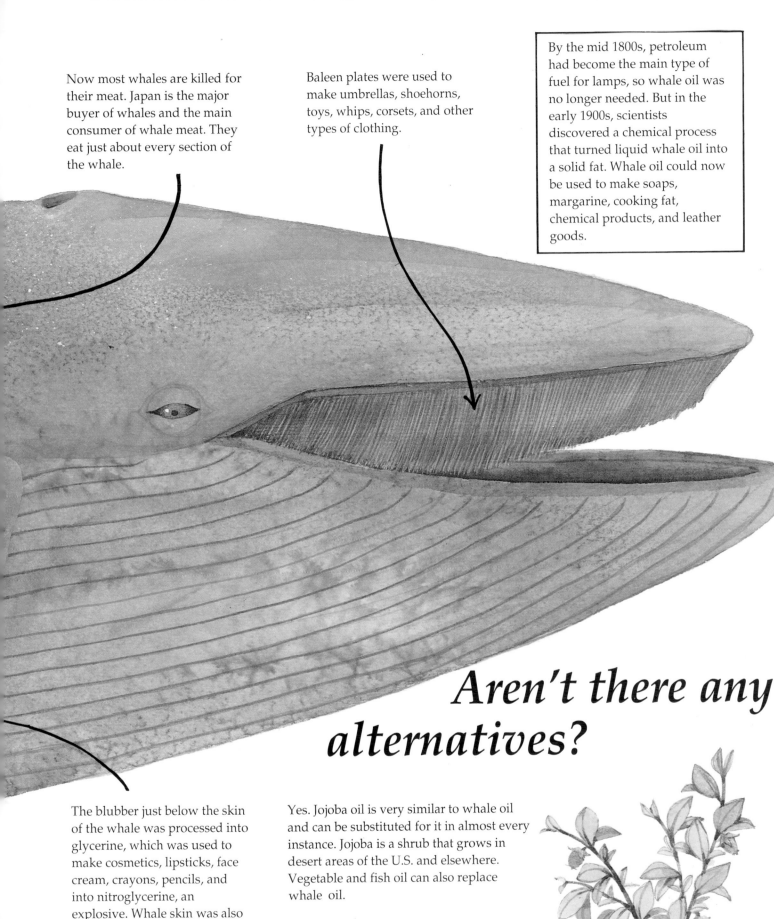

Now most whales are killed for their meat. Japan is the major buyer of whales and the main consumer of whale meat. They eat just about every section of the whale.

Baleen plates were used to make umbrellas, shoehorns, toys, whips, corsets, and other types of clothing.

By the mid 1800s, petroleum had become the main type of fuel for lamps, so whale oil was no longer needed. But in the early 1900s, scientists discovered a chemical process that turned liquid whale oil into a solid fat. Whale oil could now be used to make soaps, margarine, cooking fat, chemical products, and leather goods.

Aren't there any alternatives?

The blubber just below the skin of the whale was processed into glycerine, which was used to make cosmetics, lipsticks, face cream, crayons, pencils, and into nitroglycerine, an explosive. Whale skin was also used to make drumskins and golf bags.

Yes. Jojoba oil is very similar to whale oil and can be substituted for it in almost every instance. Jojoba is a shrub that grows in desert areas of the U.S. and elsewhere. Vegetable and fish oil can also replace whale oil.

Who are the whalers?

Many nations have at some time been involved in whaling and must share the blame for the decline of the whales. However, only a handful still kill whales for commercial uses.

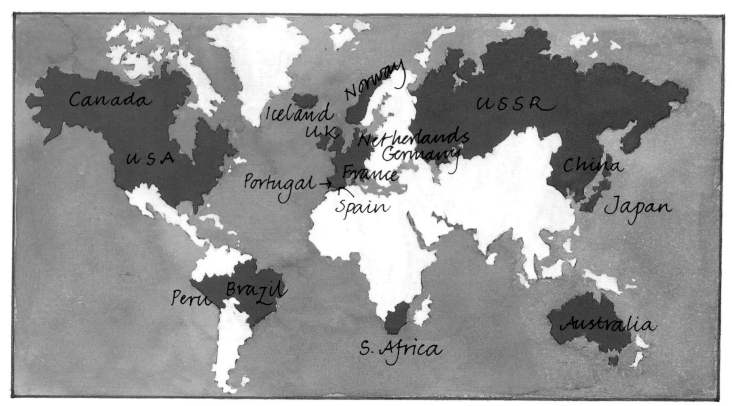

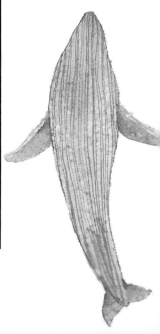

KEY

These are the major nations that were at one time actively involved in commercial whaling. All but a few have now stopped altogether.

Holland	France
Germany	Great Britain
USSR	Denmark
Portugal	Spain
US	Canada
Australia	South Africa
South Korea	China
Peru	Brazil
Norway	Japan
Iceland	

JAPAN

Since the 1960s, Japan has been the leading whaling nation. There has been pressure on them to stop, and the whalers have lowered their yearly limits from 825 minke whales to 300. But Japan still hunts whales and is the main buyer of whale meat and other whale products from other nations.

NORWAY

Norway officially stopped commercial whaling in 1988, but continued with "scientific whaling," killing a small number of minke whales each year. Norway has now decided to leave the IWC, and plans to resume commercial whaling in 1993.

ICELAND

In 1992 Iceland dropped out of the IWC and is no longer bound by its rules. They plan to return to small-scale commercial whaling of minke whales.

DENMARK (GREENLAND)

Inuits, native Greenlanders, are allowed to catch fin and minke whales as long as it is only for survival and in accordance with their local customs. People native to the Faroe Islands are allowed to catch 2,000 pilot whales, which are not covered by the IWC, in annual hunts, where they force the whales up onto the shores and kill them.

AUSTRALIA

In 1978 Australia decided to stop all whaling. It's the only country to stop because it felt that whaling was cruel and unethical. It called on all nations to stop whaling.

FRANCE

The French government is trying to convince all IWC members to make Antarctica a whale sanctuary, where whales are safe from harm. The minke whales that Japanese whalers kill live in Antarctic waters.

US

The US is the only nation that has laws it can enforce to protect whales. It can restrict access to its waters and ban imports from countries involved in whaling. Alaskan Eskimos are allowed to kill a small number of bowhead whales in keeping with their ancient traditions.

Why save the whales?

Man kills many animals for food and other uses. If we catch fish for their oil and meat, why shouldn't we hunt whales for the same reasons? Here are some reasons why whales deserve special attention:

• Whales have been hunted for so long that in some parts of the world they are nearly extinct. Their populations are now so small that it will be difficult to build up their numbers again. Local, small-scale hunting of whales allows the populations to survive, but large-scale commercial whaling will not. The existence of these creatures is at stake.

• Whales are some of the oldest animals in the world. They evolved from animals that existed 55,000,000 years ago. We can learn a lot about evolution and nature, and even about ourselves, by studying whales and their behavior.

• There are many alternatives to whale products, so killing whales on a large commercial scale is not really necessary.

• If the whales cease to exist, many marine systems will be upset. Large numbers of small animals live on the bodies of whales. Barnacles live on whales. A humpback whale can carry as much as 992 lbs. (450 kg) worth of barnacles.

• Whales reproduce slowly. They have only one baby at a time, unlike fish, who produce many offspring in each cycle. It takes several years to produce a new generation of whales.

• Whales are killed in an unusually cruel way. Sometimes it takes many harpoons or clubs to kill a whale, who will die a slow death. Some scientists think that whaling should be stopped on cruelty grounds alone.

• Whales are one example of a common resource. No one owns the world's whales, or the world's oceans. If we can't join together to keep them safe, how can we expect to keep similar common resources, such as air and water, safe as well? We have the power to save the whales. Let's use it.

One obstacle to the total protection of whales is that the IWC has no real power to enforce its rules. Countries are not obliged to belong to the IWC.

Every country, company, and individual must decide what action to take to save the whales. What can countries do? The US can restrict people from fishing in their waters and can refuse to accept fish products from whaling nations. Other countries can follow suit and can boycott the fish products and other exports of these nations. As many countries as possible must support the IWC and encourage the whaling nations to remain in the IWC.

Companies can act as well. In the 1970s Clark Shoes in Britain decided not to use sperm whale oil or any leather treated with sperm whale oil. Scientists at Clark even developed a method of testing leather for signs of sperm whale oil. Clark's actions helped move Britain and Europe toward a total ban on sperm oil and all whale products. The ban was officially adopted in 1980.

What can you do to help?

• Now that you've read this book, how do you feel about whales and the history of whaling? Do you think it is right to allow a whole species to be removed from the earth?

• If you feel that it is important to help whales, you can do more than just think about it. You can ask your parents not to buy fish and fish products from whaling nations such as Iceland and Japan. Ask them to help support alternatives to whale products, especially jojoba oil. Many shampoos and cosmetics are made from jojoba shrubs. The more these products are used, the faster scientists will work to develop ways to harvest jojoba on a commercial scale.

• You can speak for whales, so let your voice be heard. Write to the embassies of the whaling nations and tell them you think they should stop killing whales.

Office of the Ambassador
Japanese Embassy
2502 Massachusetts Avenue, N.W.
Washington, D.C. 20008

Office of the Ambassador
Icelandic Embassy
2022 Connecticut Avenue, N.W.
Washington, D.C. 20008

Office of the Ambassador
Norwegian Embassy
2720 34th Street, N.W.
Washington, D.C. 20008

You can also help support environmental groups that work to protect whales. Write these groups for information about whales and whaling, and how you can help.

Greenpeace
1436 U Street, N.W.
Washington, D.C. 20009

International Wildlife Coalition and Whale Adoption Project
564 North Falmouth Highway
North Falmouth, MA 02556

Share what you have learned about whales with others. Make a whale poster for a wall in your classroom or home. Ask your teacher to help you organize a whale day at school. You could hold a swim-a-thon to raise money for the whales.

It's now illegal to hunt blue whales, thanks to years of hard work by concerned scientists and conservationists, and growing public awareness. But other whales are still in danger. And many other animals share the blue whale's bleak history. By caring, you can help save a species from extinction, and this makes you a member of The Creature Club.

The Whaling Game

OBJECT:

You need to move your whale family from the cold Arctic waters around the playing board to your warm winter home. You must avoid the whaling fleets while searching for good feeding and birthing grounds—other whales may help you on your journey.

INSTRUCTIONS:

Copy the 12 potluck boxes to the right onto index cards and cut them out. Cut out 12 whale pieces also.

Deal each player (2 to 4 players) 3 whale pieces and 3 potluck cards. Put spare whale pieces in a whale pool to draw from later as needed. Have each player randomly place their potluck cards face down around the playing board.

Take turns rolling dice—you must roll a 6 to begin your journey. When you land on a potluck card, turn it over and follow the instructions. Leave the card where it is.

The person who gets the most whales to their winter home wins.

POTLUCK CARDS

Uh-oh! Big whaling fleet on the horizon. Go back 3 spaces.

Good luck! A Greenpeace boat escorts you ahead 2 spaces.

Oh no! Struck by a harpoon. Lose 1 member of your family.

Wounded but not killed by a whaler. Lose 1 turn.

Great feeding ground. Gain extra turn with all your new energy!

Secret birthing place where your calves are born. Add a new member to your family.

POTLUCK CARDS

Large oil spill keeps you from moving. Go back 2 spaces.

Disaster! Whaling fleet takes 2 family members. A sad day.

You hear messages from other whales who guide you safely ahead. Take extra turn.

Strange currents force you to wash up on land. Lose 1 turn.

Calm warm waters and no whalers in sight. Take extra turn.

You find whale that was stranded and lost. Add the whale to your family.

WHALE PIECES

Start

Artic 3

Whalers! Lose one family member

Pool

ter
ne

Start

Arctic 2

Index